Fen, Fire & Flood

Scenes from Fenland History

By Edward Storey

CAMBRIDGESHIRE LIBRARIES PUBLICATIONS

ISBN 0902 436414

© Cambridgeshire Libraries Publications gratefully acknowledges the
help received from:

John Baguley for use of photographs
Cambridgeshire Collection for illustrations
Mary Liquorice FLA for the Index
Peterborough City Museum & Art Gallery

Designed & Printed by Heffers Printers Limited, Cambridge

Cover illustration by Sam Thompson at Gerry Ball & Associates

Published by Cambridgeshire Libraries Publications
c/o Central Library, Broadway,
Peterborough PE1 1RX

Telephone (0733) 48343

Contents

Chapter One
TIME – JOURNEY

Can you imagine a time when this area of Britain, which we call the Fens, was more like a jungle, with wild wolves, bears, bison, sabre-toothed tigers and even the occasional hippopotamus? Can you imagine yourself walking through a primeval forest or a plague-ridden swamp and then coming face-to-face with a dinosaur, or any other prehistoric animal?

Straight-tusked elephant whose remains were found at Peterborough.
Picture courtesy of the Sedgwick Museum, Cambridge.

It is possible, with a little help from some of the descriptions you are about to read. Because of scientists, geologists, historians and writers, we now know quite a lot about the past. We now have evidence to prove that wild and unusual creatures did once roam over this part of the country where we see only lazy sheep or harmless, wide-eyed cows.

A few years ago, near one of the brickyards on the edge of the Fens, some workmen discovered the complete skeleton of a plesiosaur which was 160 million years old. The very clay from which our bricks are made was also formed millions of years earlier by the deposits of an ancient sea which once flowed over the land where your house, school, shopping centre or football ground now stand.

Fossils of prehistoric fish have been found in that clay which suggests that there was some kind of life here 500 million years ago, long before the arrival of the dinosaurs and long before the arrival of Man. Wherever we live, or whatever we do, it is important to remember that even the most ordinary place has a history of dramatic events and changes.

If we could transport ourselves to any period of Fenland history we would find ourselves in a very different landscape from that which we know today because the countryside is always changing, sometimes slowly, sometimes suddenly. Features of the landscape disappear even in our own lifetime. What is familiar to us now will appear very strange to those people who may come to settle in the Fen country in a thousand years time, just as the past is often very hard for us to understand when we look back.

Are you interested in murders, rebellions, riots, hangings, battles, fires, floods, deeds of heroism, or people like Hereward the Wake and Oliver Cromwell? If so this brief history of the Fens should appeal to you because, like most other parts of Britain, it has had plenty of drama and more than a few outstanding characters.

To get our own times into perspective let us go back to just over ten thousand years ago, when thick layers of ice still covered much of the land and the climate was more like that of the North Pole. The Fens, as we know them today, did not exist then. There was no North Sea, no English Channel, no seaside resorts like Mablethorpe, Skegness, Hunstanton or Cromer. Britain was not even an island. When our three main rivers started to form they were no

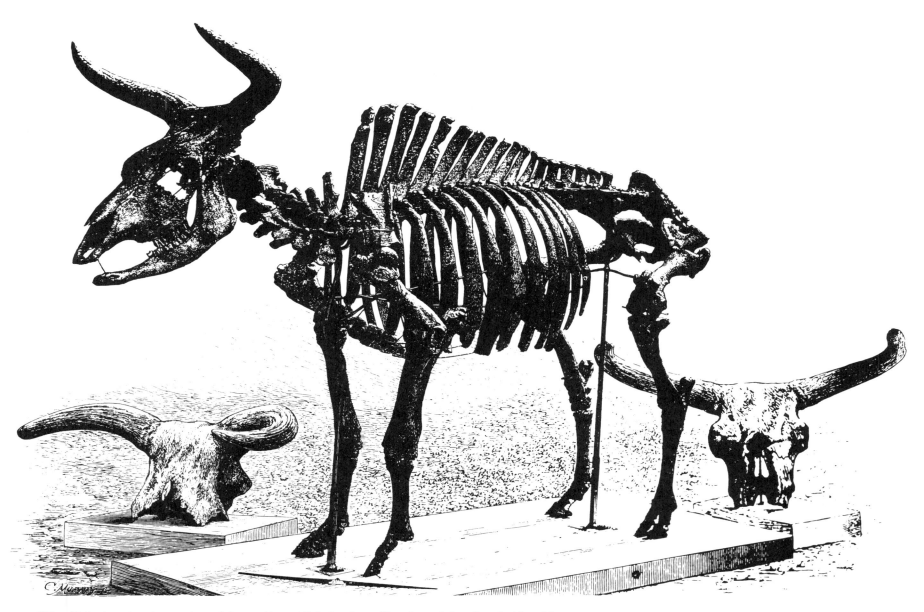

Skeleton of Bos Primigenius (ancestor of domestic cattle), in the collection of the Cambridge Museum.

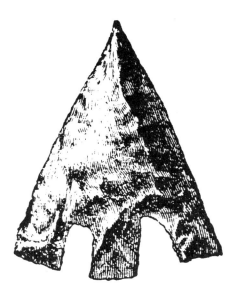

Flint arrow head
from Chatteris.

more than tributaries of the River Rhine. It is difficult for us to see the River Great Ouse, the Nene and the Welland as part of someone else's country.

But slowly, as the Ice Ages began to recede, as the vast layers of melting snow became water, some very dramatic geological changes took place and Britain began to take shape. New rivers, seas, coastlines and islands were carved out the old world. New countries were created, among them our own.

Even that episode is only a small part of the story. We also have to remember that the northern half of the Continent had known extremes of climate. Sometimes there were centuries of arctic conditions which 'put the earth to sleep' and sometimes there were centuries of tropical conditions which allowed some of those prehistoric animals to exist. And each period was carefully recorded by nature in the layers of earth that were accumulating. Animal-droppings, bones, shells, leaves, trees, flints, all preserved for later times to discover, so that we can get a glimpse into the past.

When Britain at last became an island, those primitive people who had wandered across the Continent found themselves cut off and so became the earliest settlers in a new land. Tribes were established, nations were born, kings and warriors emerged to lead the people into the future. We are the continuation of those early beginnings. History is not just some boring old thing that happened a long time ago. It is happening all the time and we are part of it.

Can you imagine yourselves, then, on a Time-journey, a journey into the past where you will get a glimpse of what life was like for those other people who lived here before us? We could find ourselves sitting round a campfire, watching a Stone Age family cooking a joint of wild boar or deer. Some of the men might be making a new set of flint tools with which to go hunting, some of the women might be making clothes out of animal skins, and the children might be playing some primitive game of marbles. Or, we might find ourselves at a Roman settlement and see there how much more sophisticated those conquerors of Britain lived their lives, introducing some of the customs and fashions from their own country.

Wherever we pause for a moment, whether it is with the Ancient Britons, Romans, Vikings or Normans, we shall see that they have all left some influence, some evidence of their presence here, which we have absorbed into our own way of life.

Because of what we learn from them we may be able to think more carefully about what we would like our contribution to be to this story which has no end.

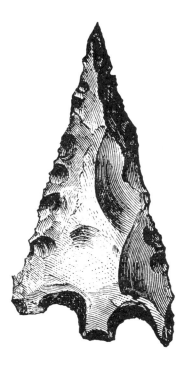

Flint arrow head from Bourne Fen.

Chapter Two
WHAT ARE THE FENS?

By the time the early Britons sorted themselves out into separate tribes and kingdoms the land of the Fen-country had started to settle down after all the upheavals of nature. The Ice-Age of ten thousand years ago had itself become part of history and these islands were cut-off from the main continental land-mass. Not until men built boats to cross the seas were we threatened by any force beyond our newly-created shores. We were on our own, fighting among ourselves as one tribe trespassed on to the territory of another.

Those jungle-like forests I told you about earlier, had largely been destroyed by hurricanes and floods over a long period of time when not even the seasons were able to make up their minds what to do next. Millions of tree trunks lay buried in the wet peat where they were to be preserved for as long as seventy-thousand years until farmers of the twentieth century discovered them when ploughing.

When you travel through the Fens today you will often see some of those ancient tree trunks piled up at the edge of a field. We call them 'bog-oaks', though they are not all oaks. Some are hazel, some fir, and some yew. For years they have been a nuisance to farmers, breaking ploughshares and damaging machines. Some trunks have been so difficult to get out of the ground that they have been blown-up with explosives. Most of the wood is very hard and for years was considered useless. Now some of our modern sculptors like to use it for carving their own creations. Imagine what it is like to hold a wooden bowl or vase which has been made out of a tree that was once growing in the Fens long before the pyramids were built in Egypt. When we can *touch* history like this it suddenly comes to life for us. We can picture a time when those trees once had leaves, when prehistoric animals searched for food beneath the branches, when primitive man went hunting for food in those dark forests.

How did all those tree trunks come to be buried so deeply in the soil, and nearly all of them facing in the same direction? The most accepted theory is that the peat caused by the decaying vegetation became so thick and damp over the years that the sap was no longer able to rise in the trees. I suppose we could say that they began to suffer from hypothermia. Their blood-supply was cut off and they started to die. The trunks slowly rotted just above the level of the peat and were finally blown down in a severe south-westerly gale and they gradually sank into the soft wet peat which they had helped to create. Strangely, that peat which had been partly responsible for destroying them also helped to preserve them for all those years.

82ft long bog oak, weighing 8 tons, found at Stretham.
Picture courtesy of Cambridge Daily News.

It is difficult for us to imagine now that the level of the land was once much higher than it is today. When most of the water was drained from the Fens in the seventeenth century the soil began to shrink. It was like squeezing the water from a bath-sponge. The sponge grew smaller and, when dry, started to waste away. If the level of that land could, by some act of magic, be restored for us at this moment it is more than likely that your School, your house, and many of the other buildings around you, would be buried as much as six-and-a-half metres deep. In some places only tall buildings and church spires would be left sticking out of the ground like jagged stones on a deserted beach. Today most of the Fens are below sea-level and if the sea-walls broke or the river-banks burst most of the countryside would be drowned.

How the land came to be like this is something we shall look at again more fully in Chapter Twelve. What we have to remember now is that these low-lands of East Anglia have always been threatened by water and even today, with all our skilful engineering, we cannot afford to neglect our rivers and drains. If we do the Fens will soon return to being a wilderness of marsh and flood. They would, in fact, revert to being true 'fen-country' once again.

Now you are probably asking 'if the fen-country still exists, how can it go back to being true fen-country?' Well, to be honest, we ought not to be calling these areas of Cambridgeshire and Lincolnshire fens any more because natural fens no longer exist. There are preserved fens, like the well-known one you can visit at Wicken, but the term we use for the rest of the land is not strictly accurate. If we look up the word in our dictionaries we shall find a fen is described as 'a low, marshy piece of land often under water; a morass or bog; an undrained marsh not fit for cultivation . . .'. That definition may have been true once, but not any more. Before the Fens were drained thousands of acres could be under water for two-thirds of the year and some areas were permanently water-logged. The only places where people could live then were on the remote islands which were scattered about like giant stepping-stones throughout the dreary wastelands.

Perhaps you have noticed that many place-names in the Fens end in *ea* or *ey*: Stonea, Manea, Thorney and Ramsey. That last syllable usually means that the place was once an island. It is difficult for us to imagine now that so many of our towns and villages were once surrounded by water, that in those far-off days people frequently went from place to place in small boats, or even on stilts. Those who used stilts were often known as 'Cambridgeshire Camels'.

When, during a hard winter, all that water was frozen the people had to find other means of transport – toboggans and skates (which we shall read about later).

What a different world it was three or four hundred years ago when our ancestors lived in a region that was mostly water – a world of reed-beds, marshes, swamps and islands, of wild-fowl, frogs, eels and fish of all descriptions.

It would be a pity if we lost the word 'Fens' from our language but you can see how much they have changed from their original description. Today the Fens are both attractive and productive, providing us with much of our food, especially potatoes, carrots, sugar-beet, celery and wheat. Our water-ways now are used by holiday-makers who like to get away from cities and enjoy the beauties of our unusual landscape.

What we have to remember is that our landscape, as we see it, is largely man-made. Most of it has, at some time, been re-

Fenland stilt walker.

claimed from the water. Men have shaped and cultivated the pattern of our fields and roads, mainly through the important drainage schemes. One of the features you will notice is the complex network of rivers, dykes and channels which criss-cross the countryside. You have only to look at those long straight waterways to realise that someone has taken a hand in reorganising nature.

However, we must not get diverted into fen-drainage yet. We must stay for a few moments on that route which led from pre-historic man to the arrival of the Roman Army, those invaders who came across the sea to civilise what they saw as a primitive and barbaric country.

What sort of Britain did those men find? What kind of land did Julius Caesar expect to conquer when he set foot on these shores in 55 BC? To begin with the native opposition was much fiercer than he thought it would be and the Roman Army was not finally successful in occupying Britain until AD 43. Some of the hardest battles were fought in East Anglia and the tradition of resistance and stubbornness in the Fens firmly established.

Example of beakerware in Peterborough Museum and Art Gallery.

Chapter Three
WHAT THE ROMANS FOUND

We have already seen how the conditions of the Fen-country changed considerably from time to time, see-sawing between dry and wet periods, making it difficult for some tribes to establish themselves in one place for any length of time.

One of the main problems, both before and after the Romans, came from the sea. The high tides would flow quite a long way up the Fen rivers but very often they could not get back again because heavy deposits of silt were constantly being left at the river out-falls. This meant that eventually the mouth of the river built up its own sea-banks and the ebbing water could no longer flow out into that great basin we now call The Wash.

Further inland the soil was subsiding, creating a vast saucer-like area into which all the flood-water flowed from the upland counties of Leicestershire, Northamptonshire, Bedfordshire and beyond. Daniel Defoe, who wrote *Robinson Crusoe*, once described the old Fens as 'the sink of thirteen counties', which was not all that flattering but very true.

Inevitably, centuries of conflict with nature bred a race of stubborn, defiant people and the Romans found a much more war-like race than they expected. We can be fairly certain that many Fenmen went to join the British army led by Queen Boadicea (properly known as Boudicca) which successfully slaughtered the Ninth Legion but, in the end, the greater might of the well-trained legionaries won the day and the whole of East Anglia had to submit to Roman rule.

Evidence of what life was like even before the Romans came is regularly being discovered in the well-organised excavations which are still going on throughout the country. Most of our museums have specimens of pots, hand-axes, arrow-heads, flints and ornaments used by the early settlers. The recent finding of a large Bronze Age settlement near Peterborough shows how these primitive people were trying to organise themselves into communities. Although it all looks very basic to us now it was, for them, a major development.

I wonder what they would say if they could make a time-journey to one of today's modern cities or shopping centres? What would they say if they could buy their joint of meat from a super-market instead of having to go out hunting for it? How would they feel about going into a fashion-shop to buy a dress or a pair of jeans, all ready to wear? Perhaps they would be so scared-stiff of all the noise, that they would scurry back to their own times where, from the wild beasts which they killed, they had to take not only the meat they needed for their food but also the skins and furs which they made into clothes. I suppose we could say that the dead animal was their 'shopping-centre'. The horns were used as drinking-cups, the bones were shaped into cutting implements, and the fat used to provide fuel for cooking and also for rush-lights. Nothing was ever wasted.

If it took those early tribes a long time to discover that they could *grow* food, it took them just as long to realise that they could *make* things from the earth, especially from the clay beneath the soil. But, fortunately, human-beings have always been experimenters and, having learned how to make fires, they eventually found how to make pottery and glass. It became quite a status-symbol then to drink from hand-made mugs or beakers. The beaker was such an important invention in eastern counties that a tribe of people who specialised in producing them became known as the Beaker people. It is interesting to think that today we are turning more and more away from mass-produced things and prefer to use pots, bowls and mugs which have been made by hand.

Already we can see how the people of two and three thousand years ago, slowly and cautiously, came to live together as communities with their own laws and ways of life, establishing the beginnings of what became our villages, towns and cities. They were not as sophisticated as we like to think *we* are and it is hard for us to appreciate that at that time there were fewer than 20,000 people living in the whole of East Anglia. Places such as Cambridge, Ely, Norwich, Bury St Edmunds and Peterborough, had populations of a few dozen families and a town of a hundred inhabitants was considered quite important.

But, as fast as these communities tried to establish themselves in the Fens, so nature tried just as hard to discourage them. As we have already noticed, Fen-people are not that easily put off and they stubbornly refused to be driven out of their land. In fact they became so used to living in a wild and watery countryside that they were to resent anyone who tried to change it for them. They were

Model of Bronze Age village.

Picture courtesy of Peterborough Development Corporation.

skilled at catching fish, eels and wild ducks, and could use the reeds and mud for building. They also felt safer in what they knew to be a very inhospitable land to everyone else.

We must give the Romans credit for realising that if only the land could be properly drained it would provide very fertile soil for crops. They saw that it was necessary to build good roads, to cut dykes across the fields, and to strengthen the sea-banks against the high tides.

Much of their work can still be traced today. One of the most famous examples is the Carr Dyke, a canal built through miles of boggy ground. 'Carr' is an old Norse word for 'a meadow recovered by drainage from the fen'. When the Carr Dyke was in use it was estimated to be one hundred and thirty kilometres long and stretched from Waterbeach in Cambridgeshire to Witham in Lincolnshire. It is still possible to walk along part of its banks north of Peterborough and on a quiet summer's day you can imagine the Roman soldiers camped under our great Fenland sky.

The purpose of the Carr Dyke may not have been just to drain the land but also to provide a more convenient method of transporting provisions to those Legions which were now occupying much of the north. Many waterways existed before the roads were built and it was often more efficient to link them together with new canals and then transport supplies by boat rather than horse and waggon.

The Fenmen of the seventeenth century were to refuse to work for Cornelius Vermuyden but the people of the first century had no choice. The Romans were the occupying forces and could make the local people do all the manual labouring for them, just like slaves. One of the Roman reporters at that time, a man called Tacitus, wrote: 'The Britons complained that the Romans wore out and consumed their bodies and hands in clearing the woods and embanking the Fens'. It was not uncommon for these local labour-gangs to work fifteen hours a day in all weathers, digging and building the dykes and sea-defences, and eventually the roads.

Under foreign rule the shape of England was beginning to change. Wastelands were turned into farms. Crops began to grow on land which had once been under water. New towns were established near the Roman garrisons.

The authority of the Roman rulers in England did not last. The mighty military Legions who had one marched triumphantly across the land were now dispersed and many of them had been recalled to their own country, leaving the less able troops behind to control the natives of this extreme part of their empire. Many of the fine villas which were built by the Romans soon became ruins and much of the drainage work in the Fens was neglected. Gradually nature took over and the fields returned to a state of wildness, with floods, marshes, misty swamps and fevers. The miserable and dispirited people retreated to their camps and, on what higher ground they could find, lived out the winter in small huts. By the end of the fifth century the area had become almost forgotten, a hide-out for robbers, murderers, outlaws and small tribes of people who had survived not only the Roman invasion but also their own internal wars.

A new breed of fen-dweller was in the making.

Carr Dyke.   *Picture courtesy of John Baguley.*

Chapter Four
THE VIKINGS ARRIVE

The only surviving strongholds of civilisation in this country for the next five or six hundred years were the religious foundations – the communities of monks who established themselves on the isolated islands in the Fens, where they now felt reasonably safe.

Since Christianity had been brought to England these men had quietly but deliberately been gaining power. They built their abbeys, or monasteries, on the best land they could find and saw it as their right to use the labour of any villagers nearby. They cultivated gardens, grew their own grapes for making wine, bred sheep and cattle (even though many of them chose not to eat meat), and charged high rents for the manors which they let to the thanes or noblemen of the area.

Like all religious communities their chief aim was to further the study and practice of Christianity, to pray and to worship, to write books and to serve the needs of others. But the abbeys became very wealthy and, because of their wealth, they were to be one of the main attractions to other invaders who were preparing to cross the North Sea and plunder this land.

By the eighth and ninth centuries many of these abbeys had already become prosperous places – Ely, Ramsey, Thorney, Sawtry, Crowland and Peterborough (which at the time was known as Medeshamsted). Even when they were burnt down or destroyed they were rebuilt on an even larger and more spectacular scale. Some are now no more than ruins. Others, like Ely and Peterborough, still survive as part of the Cathedral buildings and give us some idea what an abbey was like between the twelfth and fifteenth centuries.

One of the most appealing episodes in the history of Fenland monasteries took place in the seventh century and concerned a young Mercian nobleman called Guthlac. He had grown tired of the constant battles between the various kingdoms and decided that he would much rather be a monk, living a peaceful and useful life instead of a wasteful and destructive one. Guthlac first went to the monastery at Repton but found that life there was far too comfortable and undemanding. So he made his way over to East Anglia and the monastery at Thorney. But even there he felt that the monks were living rather too well and the discipline did not offer him the challenge he needed. So, on 24th August, 699, he persuaded two of the Thorney monks to row him over to a neighbouring island at Crowland – which was then spelt Crulande, meaning a 'crude, rough and boggy land'.

Crowland had a reputation for being a particularly horrible place. In his fear and loneliness Guthlac believed that he was being

St. Guthlac's Cross near Crowland. Inscription reads 'Guthlac has placed this stone for his boundary mark'.

persecuted by gangs of men with big ugly heads, long necks, bearded faces, fierce eyes and stinking breath. He was sure that they had fire spitting from their mouths and their harsh, terrifying screams seemed to echo all night under the black menacing sky. Although the local people might have been suspicious of this strange little hermit living alone in his hut, it is more likely that all Guthlac was really suffering from was a nasty fever and the occasional nightmare. Fen ague or fever was a common complaint in those days in areas of undrained marshland. Eventually his fears subsided and he began to earn for himself a reputation as a very gentle young man who cared for the people who lived nearby, healed all kinds of sickness, and even tamed wild animals. There's a nice story about him which says that when the first swallows arrived back in this country in the spring they would always go to perch on Guthlac's shoulder first to find out where they could build their nests.

His fame spread and it was not long before he began to receive visitors from other parts of the country. One day a nobleman called Ethelbald came to see him and Guthlac prophesied that this man would be crowned king of Mercia. Ethelbald could not believe that this would be possible and said to the monk that if such an honour was ever bestowed upon him he would build a fine new monastery at Crowland to express his gratitude.

Guthlac's prophecy came true but, sadly, not in his own lifetime. He died at the age of forty in AD 714. Two years later, Ethelbald (now the crowned king of Mercia) gave instructions for the building of a monastery on the island where he had first met the saintly hermit.

Although Saint Guthlac was never to be forgotten, the new abbey was destroyed and burnt down, not just once but several times. First by the Vikings and then much later by the troops of Oliver Cromwell, when it has already been reduced to a parish church.

The Vikings were responsible for ransacking most of the monasteries in the eastern half of England between the ninth and tenth centuries. An historian called Hugh Candidus, a monk at Peterborough Abbey, writing in the twelfth century of these troubled times of the Viking invasion, left this vivid description:

'then came the Danes, servants of the Devil, and like mad dogs and robbers issuing of a sudden from their dens, even so they land of a sudden from their ships and come on a people that suspected no evil, burning cities, villas, young men, women and children . . . all things they consume with robbery, fire and swords, taking care that none should live to bring tidings of this massacre . . .'

Standing in the ruins of Crowland Abbey on a misty day it is not difficult to imagine those dragon-headed long-boats slowly making their way up the Fenland rivers to within sight of the abbey buildings, the Vikings mooring their boats in the tall reeds, silently stealing along the river-banks and then, screaming and wielding their swords, setting light to the buildings and brutally murdering the inhabitants.

At Crowland all the monks were killed except two, who escaped. The Abbot Theodore, who was kneeling at the altar praying for his

"Guthlac builds his church."—Illustration from a 12th century manuscript containing pictures in the life of St. Guthlac.

15

Crowland Abbey.   *Picture courtesy of John Baguley.*

attackers, was suddenly stabbed through the head with a long sword and left to die on the altar steps. Until recently his skull could be seen in a glass case inside the abbey, a grim reminder of those violent days.

One of the main reasons for the abbeys being attacked was their wealth. They possessed precious jewels, silver and gold plates, and a great amount of money in their treasuries. They were certainly the richest places in the Fens and were as prosperous as the dukes and lords who owned the rest of England. When the Vikings discovered how wealthy the abbeys were they came to plunder them time and time again. The abbeys were not only easy to reach by boat, they were also undefended.

At Crowland they also destroyed one of the finest libraries in the kingdom. Over a thousand beautiful volumes of illuminated manuscripts went up in flames. Not even the villagers escaped. They too were murdered so that, as Hugh Candidus said, 'none should live to bring tiding of this massacre'.

The same scene of terror was repeated wherever there was a religious building. At Peterborough the Vikings raised such a fire that it burnt the whole city to the ground and all the monks, and many of the townspeople, perished. It was a threat which was to last for another hundred years and it was common to hear people pray then 'From the Norsemen, Good Lord, deliver us'.

Some of the Vikings' long-boats have actually been found buried in the Fens. One was unearthed at Manea some years ago but the people did not know what it was and chopped it up for firewood! But, as always happens after a period of hostility and war, many of the invaders became settlers in this country and helped to improve the standard of living in the Fens and the north of England. Many people believed that they were better masters than the Romans and even better masters than the autocractic abbots of the Church. As the Danes began to cultivate the land which they now occupied so they introduced into the country several new crafts. They were not all barbarians. Eventually they brought their wives and families over to live with them and a new culture, with different traditions and skills, was added to those which already existed. The Vikings were particularly fine craftsmen in silver, metal and wood, and we can see many examples of their work now in the brooches and necklaces displayed in our museums.

Chapter Five
AN UNCERTAIN PEACE

One of the Danish noblemen who became a legend was King Canute and his name is still remembered in several parts of the Fens in such places as King's Delph, King's Dyke and Canute Drove. He was once so impressed by the beautiful singing he heard coming from Ely monastery one day, as he was sailing on the river, that he encouraged all the abbeys to improve their music so that others could enjoy the same pleasure. An old rhyme records that occasion:

'Merrily sang they, the monks at Ely,
When Canute the King he rowed thereby;
Row to the shore, men, said the King
And let us hear these monks to sing.'

Eventually, instead of monotonous chanting, the monks introduced a variety of musical ideas into their worship and there are those who see King Canute as one of the 'fathers of English Church music'. As well as visiting Ely he also went to Ramsey Abbey and Peterborough. To have travelled by boat from Peterborough to Ramsey in those days would have meant crossing Whittlesey Mere, an inland stretch of water which was about the size of Lake Derwentwater in Cumbria. The Mere had a reputation for violent and unexpected storms and King Canute was not very eager to sail on it for fear of being shipwrecked or drowned. So he ordered a new river to be cut through the Fens to enable him to sail more safely from one place to another. This, we believe, is how King's Dyke and King's Delph, near Whittlesey, came to have their names and the narrow waterway on which Canute sailed a thousand years ago can still be seen today.

As England tried to settle down again after the Danish invasions the ordinary people had to get used to new ways of working and new systems of law. No nation stands still and the people of England were once again trying to cultivate their land, to grow what crops they could, to improve their houses and to come to terms with their

Remains of original Peterborough Abbey.

new rulers. Now that an uncertain peace had been restored they planned for the future. Towns and villages increased their populations, different breeds of cattle were to be seen in the fields and some of the new skills brought over by the Vikings were now taken for granted.

The monks, too, began the laborious task of rebuilding their monasteries, not with wood, clay and wattle this time, but with stone. Much of the stone for the new abbeys of the Fens was excavated from the massive stone-quarries at Barnack near Stamford. It was cut and hauled away from the site by teams of bullocks and the labourers then loaded it on to barges so that it would be transported to wherever it was needed. Peterborough, Ramsey, Crowland, Thorney, Sawtry, Bury St Edmunds and many other places in the Fens built their abbeys and churches of Barnack stone. Today the extinct quarries are grassed over and the area a Nature Conservancy site, better known for its wildflowers and as a place for picnics.

Many of the religious Orders came over from the Continent and some from Ireland, their names depending on which saint the monks adopted as their founder. The Benedictines – named after St Benedict – were the strongest Order in the Fens but there were also Cistercians and Augustinians. Each Rule tried to be better and more prosperous than the others and there was a lot of quarrelling going on between them in those early days.

Although Christianity had been firmly established as the new religion by the year AD 800, the ambitious programme of rebuilding many of the abbeys did not take place until after the Norman Conquest. What was already clearly apparent at this time was the power of the abbeys. Abbots became as powerful as kings and the Archbishop of Canterbury could exercise as much authority as any man who sat on the throne of England. In fact the reigning monarchs in succession gave vast sums of money to the Church. Some abbeys were given whole villages. When Ramsey Abbey was founded the king gave it precious jewels and silver, plus the parish of Godmanchester with all its rents and revenues.

It was only natural that such power and wealth should create resentment among the people. Many could remember that it was originally because of the abbeys' riches that Fenland villages were destroyed and their inhabitants killed. While they and their children starved the monks often enjoyed a good standard of living, with plenty of food, wine and warmth.

Bitter disputes frequently broke out between the abbeys themselves as they quarrelled and fought over the possession or ownership of land. It was not the religion itself which was wrong but the way in which it was used by its followers for their own greed. Not all abbots were guilty of this kind of behaviour. Some, like Crowland, were well-known for their charity and good works, for their learning and humility. There is an old Fenland rhyme which sums up the reputation of each abbey:

'Ramsey the rich of gold and fee,
Thorney the flower of many fair tree,
Crowland the courteous of meat and drink,
Spalding the gluttons as all men do think.
Peterborough the proud as all men say,
Sawtry, by the way, that old abbey
Gave more alms in one day than all they.'

What we also have to remember is that a thousand years ago the monks were almost the only people who could read and write. Not even our kings were as well educated and the monks' knowledge gave them considerable authority in the land. The origins of some of our universities can be traced back to those religious foundations and some colleges still belong to the cathedral diocese which has replaced the abbey.

By the eleventh century the country had developed sufficiently to become involved in political intrigue and to be coveted by other nations. This time it was the Normans. If the Roman and Danish invasions had changed life in England, the Norman Conquest was to have an even greater impact.

But, as so often happens in history at the time of a crisis, a figure emerges who becomes the hero of the people. In 1940, at the time of the Second World War, it was Winston Churchill. In AD 1066 it was Hereward the Wake, a man who was feared, loved, admired and despised, and who became one of the great characters of our history.

Chapter Six
HERO, OR VILLAIN?

The heroic deeds of Hereward the Wake are still argued about nine hundred years after his death and he has become such a colourful figure that we sometimes think of him as an earlier version of Robin Hood, even a myth. But he was real and he did exist.

Hereward was born on the edge of the Fens, in the small market town of Bourne in Lincolnshire and was rightly called the last great *English* warrior for his tremendously courageous fight against the Normans in the defence of Ely.

Hereward has been described as tall, with fair hair and fierce grey eyes, extremely strong but also very sensitive and charming. He is said to have liked music – he could sing and play the harp – and was a great favourite with the ladies. But he was, above all, a soldier and a born leader.

Long before he became involved in the affairs of the Fen-country's struggles he had fought campaigns in Ireland, Cornwall and Flanders. Wherever he went he earned a reputation for his bravery and his strategic skills in battle. He was a commando-type soldier who preferred to fight with small bands of men and take the enemy by surprise. He had already proved what a successful leader he was by the time he took up the cause of the Saxons against the

Alleged site of Hereward's Castle at Bourne.

Normans in the Isle of Ely.

As so often happens in the life of such a person, the time was right for him to emerge as the champion of a cause. When Edward the Confessor died in 1066 he left no rightful heir to the throne. The country was without a natural successor and the people wondered who would become their king. Edward had always had a good relationship with the Normans and had promised the throne of England to his second cousin, William of Normandy. But this was easier said than done. There were many English noblemen who felt that the king's brother-in-law, Harold, should become their new ruler. Their refusal to *give* the throne to William resulted in the famous Battle of Hastings, which Harold lost.

The only part of the kingdom which still defied William the Conqueror was the Fens. Because of their wild nature, with their meres, swamps and winding rivers, they had become a place of refuge for all those who rebelled against authority, and especially against the Norman king. Several hundred Anglo-Saxon guerilla-fighters were determined to resist these latest invaders, but they needed a leader. Hereward was their man. He had a personal vendetta against the Normans and was zealously patriotic when it came to defending his own lands. He hated the Normans so much that he was even prepared to assist the Danes in attacking the great Fenland abbeys which were about to be taken over by the French abbots.

In 1069 he personally led the Danes in an attack on Peterborough Abbey (which had been known as Medeshamstede and Gildenburch – or the Golden Borough – because of its great wealth) so that it should not fall into the hands of the Normans. After killing those monks who tried to defend the abbey, the Danes stole a gold crown and many priceless jewels from the holy cross at the high altar, and then took chests of silver from the Treasury. Finally they set fire to the buildings and hurried back to their boats on the River Nene with as much loot as they could carry.

Now, you might think that this was an unnecessary and ruthless way of showing patriotism, but it proves what a hot-headed and vicious person Hereward could be when angered. Nothing could stop him when he had made up his mind. He was impulsive and arrogant, fanatical and loyal. He was prepared to behave in exactly the same way to defend Ely if ever the Normans threatened to take it.

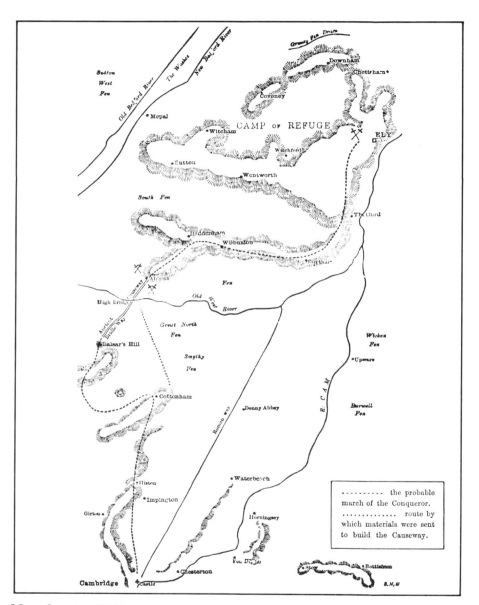

Map showing William the Conqueror's approach to Ely.

Fortunately, Ely was still guarded by loyal and militant monks who were well-armed. They had already taken the precaution of allowing into the abbey more than one hundred hand-picked soldiers – Saxon knights and Danish warriors, who knew every inch of the land. They had plenty of food, plenty of wine, enough weapons and enough time. They could see anyone approaching from miles around and believed they were safe from any attack.

William the Conqueror knew that in order to crush the resistance in the Fens he would have to capture Ely. The main problem was in getting his troops and their equipment over such boggy and uncharted ground. So, he began to build camps on those 'islands' within the Isle of Ely from which he planned to construct a causeway. From this vantage point he could then attack the city itself. This causeway was built mainly of large tree trunks fastened together with cow-hides and kept in place by huge stones. But,

Cathedral and City of Ely.

when his men tried to cross it, the construction gave way and many of them were drowned.

The King's generals were advised to try again from a different direction but Hereward learned of their plans by disguising himself as a travelling potter. When he realized what the Normans were planning to do he immediately came up with his own ideas to teach them a lesson. A similar type of 'ground-bridge' was built to cross the wide stretch of marshland around Ely. It reached for over a mile through reed-beds and deep meres. Hereward waited until the causeway was finished and the Norman soldiers were marching across it, then, with his own men hidden in the reeds, and with the wind behind them, he gave instructions for the Fen to be set alight.

Within minutes the whole length of the causeway was a sea of flames and William's army was engulfed in a tide of fire. Their screams echoed over the Fens and could be heard in Ely. Hundreds of highly-trained soldiers were slaughtered without ever putting up a fight. Those who did escape were soon caught and put to death by the sword.

Hereward's cunning and ruthlessness had won again, at least for the time being. What happened next is a bit of a mystery. It is believed that some of the Ely monks, tired of the Saxon and Danish soldiers' company and sympathetic towards the new king, allowed some of the Conqueror's men into the abbey by a secret passageway, where they were able to overthrow the drunken men who were supposed to be on guard, and then admit those who were meant to be kept out.

And so the defenders of the Isle of Ely were finally betrayed by those they were trying to defend. Hereward, bitter and outraged, fled for safety. But not for long. Eventually he was caught and thrown into prison. Several years later, and after much negotiation, he finally made peace with the Norman king and retired to his old estates in Lincolnshire.

Some historians believe that he was later murdered by a Frenchman who still hated him for what he had done to the Norman's cause. Others believed that he died a natural death and was buried in Crowland Abbey with his wife, Torfrida. Whichever is right, nothing can alter the fact that Hereward the Wake was a great soldier who fought nobly for any cause which he thought was right.

Chapter Seven
THE NEW REGIME

The Norman Conquest introduced many changes to a country which had been savaged by the Vikings and left in a state of turmoil with barons and landowners fighting over their rights. The standard of life for most ordinary people was very poor. Disease and ill-health meant that many of them died before they were thirty years old. If you were a peasant you were looked upon as just another possession of the squire or lord on whose land you happened to live, no more important than his cattle or hunting-dogs. You would not have been worth counting in the assessing of the country's population. You would have had no rights, no privileges, no votes, no medical care.

One of the first great achievements of the Normans in establishing their superiority in England was the compiling of the Domesday Book – a survey made in 1086 of all the people and places in the country with titles, lands and possessions, including their slaves, so that the king had a complete record of his new kingdom. It was the first time that such a thorough and total census had been conducted. It also meant that it was now possible for the new regime to impose and collect taxes from the people.

During this period of reorganisation most of the land previously owned by the Saxons was confiscated by the Crown and redis-

Cambridge Castle from an engraving for the Lady's Magazine.

tributed among the Norman aristocracy, many of whom had decided to settle in the counties they had fought for. Those Saxon landowners who were allowed to stay on as tenants had to vow their allegiance to the new king and promise to provide him with weapons and an army of men at any time of military threat from anyone else.

But, although the Normans did so much to change our laws and our society, they are remembered as much today for some of the great cathedrals which they built. With England now firmly related to Europe, and with the Church dedicated to Rome, there was a splendid opportunity for the wealthy to indulge in an extravagant building programme. Where better to display all the skills of the finest sculptors, artists and builders to be found in Europe than in the new churches?

Suddenly this country began to see buildings rising on a scale it had never seen before. Buildings of great vision, size, dignity and wonder. Many of them still stand and are in regular use today. When you think that these remarkable places were built by hand, with extremely primitive equipment, you can understand why we look upon them as such marvellous achievements. Many additions and improvements have inevitably been made over the years and you can often see several different styles of architecture in one building, but the Normans must take much of the credit for what we now look upon as our heritage. Without their inspiration and example we would not have had such splendours.

There were many things which were not so popular. As well as cathedrals the new rulers found it necessary to build castles. You would have thought that with all the land available in the eleventh century that there would have been no need to pull down houses to make room for these new fortifications. But, of course, the Normans wanted their castles to be in the most prominent position – usually at the gateway to a town – and this often meant demolishing part of the existing buildings. For instance, twenty-seven houses were knocked down in Cambridge to make way for the king's castle on the hill. Much the same happened at Ely and Wisbech. Understandably the local people were upset and resentful.

Something else which changed was our language. Few of the Normans were prepared to speak what was then the English language and they stubbornly insisted that French words should be

A section from the Magna Carta.

substituted wherever possible. Many old English words disappeared altogether and gradually the Britons had to compromise over the two languages if they wished to communicate. You may think that this was a good idea, that our language was enriched by the influence of another. We certainly use a lot of French words today without even thinking of their origin. They have become part of everyday speech, whether we know that language or not: pork (porc); beef (boeuf); sausage (saucisse); blouse (blouson); perfume (parfum); chair (chaire); dungeon (donjon) and chivalry (chevalerie) – a word brought over by French Knights. So, throughout the eleventh and twelfth centuries, there were periods of great reorganisation and development.

Wars of one kind or another continued to plague the country for a hundred years and the Fens were always to be a source of trouble, especially to whichever king was on the throne of England. In 1109 Henry I appointed a bishop of Ely to help bring the Fens under control but he did not succeed for long. In 1142 King Stephen found that the city had been fortified against him by Geoffrey de Mandeville and much of the land which had been taken by the Crown at the time of William the Conqueror was won back by the wealthy landowners of the Fens. King John had to ask for French troops to come over and help him fight against the barons of the Isle of Ely.

King John must have hated the Fens for it was mainly because of their barons that he was made to sign the Magna Carta and it was in the Fens that he lost his treasure, which has never been traced to this day.

If the Domesday Book is considered one of the most important documents in Britain, the Magna Carta must be another. The landowners of East Anglia were growing increasingly uneasy over the demands of King John for more taxation, more men for his armies, and for greater allegiance. They saw that the freedom of the individual, as well as the freedom of the Church, were being threatened, and Fenmen have always prided themselves on their independence. Resistance to the king's power and total authority quickly gained support and the noblemen who held the greatest influence in the Fens insisted that a Great Charter of privileges should be drawn-up and approved by the king under his personal seal. This historic document was eventually signed at Runnymede on 15th June 1215 and King John was grateful to get out of the clutches of the barons to fight the Scottish Army then invading the north.

King John lost his treasure in The Wash as he crossed from Norfolk into Lincolnshire. The Wash came much further inland than it does today but the water was often shallow and, at low tide, it was possible to cross from one county to the other in reasonable safety. However, the tides were unpredictable unless you knew every mood of the North Sea. As the king and his army made their ways across the mud-flats of that wide estuary they soon got themselves stuck and were overwhelmed by a high tide racing in over the salt marshes. Many of the king's men were drowned and the wagons carrying all his wealth vanished into the muddy water.

Today's coastline is much further east and most of that area which belonged to the sea in King John's time is now fertile land where modern farmers grow their crops. But somewhere under that land the king's jewels and treasures are still buried.

King John stag hunting.

Chapter Eight
THE BISHOP'S FORK

Although the Romans had tried to introduce a drainage system into the Fens during their occupation – with some success – their work had been sadly neglected by the Saxons and was of no immediate concern to the Normans. Consequently, the dykes which had not been maintained were now overgrown, the rivers had been allowed to silt-up and break their banks, and once against vast areas of the Fen-country reverted to marshlands, with muddy meres, boggy morasses and miles of reed-beds. All this was very fine for fishing, wild-fowling and hunting, but hopeless for agriculture and building. It was also a very damp and unhealthy climate for the people who lived there.

The only places which were habitable became islands and the people on them were forced into being isolated communities who resented strangers. They often fought among themselves and one family married into another so that nearly everyone was related to

Fen slodgers.

everyone else. They became a surly race of people who, for centuries, retained a reputation for being unfriendly.

Because of the climate they nearly all suffered from some kind of rheumatism or ague, which was rather like malaria and made them shiver with hot and cold sensations as they lay in bed. Some of the medicines they took for these illnesses would not be allowed today but, as they had no doctors, they cured themselves with whatever remedies they knew. Sometimes these included laudanum, a crude type of opium made from white poppies. It was not uncommon to see people with twisted and deformed bones, bent over almost double as they walked the village streets.

Getting from one place to another was also a problem and many families owned a flat-bottomed punt which they made from local materials, or, as we have seen, went about on long stilts. Neither the punts nor the stilts were much good in hard winter weather when the water turned to ice. Then the Fenmen had to think of other ways of getting about and skates were the answer. They were not the sophisticated skates we are used to seeing these days on ice-rinks or skating championships. To begin with they were usually made out of animal bones and strapped on to the boots. Later, some of the village blacksmiths became well-known for making iron skates at their forge as well as horseshoes. The skates were not always shaped into long and pointed blades, like they are now. Sometimes they were round, like pastry-cutters, and were worn especially by older people who would not have been able to keep their balance on the narrow blade.

Between the thirteenth and fifteenth centuries the Fens had far more water than they could hold. The meres grew bigger and fields stayed drowned for most of the year as rivers overflowed their banks. One of the problems was that no one had enough sense to co-ordinate what efforts were being made to control the problem. Landowners were inclined to be very selfish people and tried to drain their own land without worrying too much about flooding someone else's.

High tides along the east coast were now able to break much further inland, pushing the river water back upstream and making it impossible for the surplus water to flow out into the Wash. The town of Wisbech was just one of the many places which was virtually destroyed in the thirteenth century. Exceptionally high tides were recorded in 1236 and 1260, and there are accounts of hundreds of people buried during these times, who were victims of the floods. Sheep and cattle were drowned in their thousands. Dead whales were even washed upon the quay at Wisbech and nearby cottages were swept away like sand-castles.

Something had to be done and, in 1258, a committee was formed to discuss ways of draining the Fens. It worked under the not very romantic name of The Commissioners of Sewers and its main task was to organise the repair of existing drains and to make new ones. But, as always, money was needed for such work and the

Skaters on fen drain from an illustration by J. M. Heathcote, 1876.

landowners were reluctant to pay voluntary taxes into a drainage fund. Wardens were appointed to inspect all dykes and to impose fines on any owners who neglected to keep their dykes clean or who allowed their cattle to damage the river banks. There was a lot of bribery and excuses made for failing to pay taxes or protect the land and it took more than one hundred and fifty years before the Commissioners of Sewers won an Act of Parliament which enabled them to officially collect taxes from the landowners and punish those who refused to pay. Meanwhile the land went on flooding.

Morton's Leam.

One man who did do something positive about it was the Bishop of Ely – John Morton. He was not a man to argue with and had a reputation for getting his way in most things – especially the collecting of taxes. It was said that as Privy Councillor he devised a tax system which no one could dodge. If people dressed in smart clothes and looked well-off he claimed that they could afford to pay whatever taxes the State demanded. If they dressed shabbily and looked very poor, he said it was because they were mean and dishonest, having amassed large fortunes which the Exchequer had the right to claim. Rich or poor, no one escaped. Sooner or later they were caught on one of the tines (or prongs) of the Bishop's 'fork'. This image of him became so popular it was common to refer to this double tax system as Morton's Fork. Today there is a public-house in Whittlesey called *Morton's Fork* to remind us of his crafty reputation.

But it was this same Bishop who decided that he would do something practical about the continual flooding in his diocese of Ely and he decided to straighten out the narrow winding River Nene which then flowed through Stanground, Ramsey and March. Between 1487 and 1490 his labour force cut a direct route from Stanground to Guyhirn, twelve miles long, so that water could flow in a straight channel rather than the natural twisting route it usually took between the river banks. He even built a tall tower at Guyhirn so that he could personally supervise the work being done by his poorly paid navvies. His idea proved successful at the time and was taken up much later by the Dutchman, Cornelius Vermuyden in the seventeenth century.

The problem then, as now, was far too big for one man to solve and despite Bishop Morton's achievement much of the rest of the Fen country was still subject to flooding for several months of the year. Later a new and wider cut was made from Peterborough to Guyhirn and this is popular now with people who like to spend some of their holidays on the water. The River Nene, as we know it today, is very much the work of Man and quite different from the route of the Old Nene before the drainage engineers straightened it out.

The same thing has happened to our other main rivers, such as The Great Ouse and the Welland. Wherever you see a long straight stretch of water you can be sure it is where nature has been made to give in to the demands of Man.

Chapter Nine
TALES OF A GRAVE-DIGGER

You may be wondering how a grave-digger suddenly appears in this story, but it is through him that we learn about two important incidents in English history which also have their place in the history of the Fens.

The grave-digger's name was Robert Scarlett, or Old Scarlett as he is more commonly known. He is famous because he was the man who buried two queens in the cathedral at Peterborough – Katharine of Aragon, who was the first wife of Henry VIII, and Mary Stuart, Queen of Scots who was beheaded at Fotheringhay.

If you visit the cathedral at Peterborough you will find a wall-painting of Old Scarlett just inside the west door, on your left hand side as you look from the main doors towards the altar at the east end. That faded painting gives you some idea of what he must have looked like and is, I think, better than the framed picture on the opposite wall.

Old Scarlett was born in 1496 and grew to be a man of whom it was said that he was 'second to none for strength and sturdy limb'. He wore knee-length trousers made of leather with buckled leggings, and a scarlet tunic to go with his name. He had a very loud voice and was probably the town-crier as well as the sexton.

Years ago, long before newspapers or television were invented, people relied on the news being brought round the village by the town-crier – a man who would ring a hand-bell to call every one's attention to the news, or new laws which had just been passed by the king. The town-crier usually had one or two other jobs as well, such as grave-digger, bell-ringer and handyman. A sexton is just another name for a grave-digger.

Old Scarlett lived long enough to boast that he had not only buried two queens in the same building but that he had buried most of the people who died in Peterborough during his lifetime. As he lived to be ninety-eight he often joked that he had buried the dead of the city twice over – once for their own funerals and again when he had to bury their bones somewhere else to make room for the next generation.

But it is for burying the two queens that he is mostly remembered now. He became a grave-digger at the remarkably early age of

Old Scarlett, celebrated sexton of Peterborough.

Execution of Mary, Queen of Scots from an engraving by Francis Delaram.

twelve and used to boast that he was as good as any man three times his age.

Queen Katharine (or Catherine, as her name is now often spelt) died at Kimbolton Castle on 7th January, 1536 after being imprisoned there by Henry VIII following their divorce. After resting one night in Sawtry Abbey her body was brought to Peterborough for burial on 29th January. She was fifty-one and died without being allowed to see her only daughter.

Katharine came to England as a Spanish princess to marry Prince Arthur, Henry's brother. Sadly, Prince Arthur died soon after the marriage and the young Spanish princess was expected to marry her husband's brother to honour the agreement made between Spain and England.

She had always been a very popular queen with the people of this country, introducing and encouraging several new crafts, such as lace-making and embroidery to the English ladies. Many of their husbands wanted to take up arms in her honour and overthrow the king when he divorced her, but she said that she would never want to be responsible for shedding a single drop of English blood and so forbade the soldiers to pursue their plans.

When she died the king commanded that she should not be treated as a queen, only as a princess dowager. He refused to allow her to be buried in London and, as well as refusing her request to see her daughter, he also said she should be buried without any mourners. But the nation was deeply shocked at her death and hundreds of loyal subjects made their way to Peterborough to pay homage to her memory.

They lined the streets and watched the great procession of nearly five hundred mourners pass through the Norman Gateway into the Cathedral Precincts. The bell boomed out its solemn note as the coffin arrived on a wagon which was draped in black velvet trimmed with gold. The six horses which pulled the coffin were also dressed in black cloth which hung down to the ground. Sixteen priests in white surplices rode on horseback, with a gold cross carried before them. Then came the queen's personal ladies-in-waiting and the Court officers, each wearing their coat-of-arms. There were ten heralds carrying torches and a hundred and fifty servants, all walking to the mournful throb of the muffled drums.

Inside the cathedral (or abbey as it was then called) the lead coffin was placed on a catafalque, just like a royal coffin would be today in Westminster Hall. On the day that Queen Katharine was buried three bishops took it in turn to say the Mass and more than five hundred people stood in the congregation which packed the nave. The great stone pillars on either side were draped with the banners of several other countries, who were also represented by their ambassadors.

By the end of the day more than a thousand candles were burning around the coffin and prayers were said continually for the soul of the beloved queen. Finally her body was lowered into the grave which had been prepared for her by Old Scarlett.

The other queen – Mary, Queen of Scots – did not have such an impressive funeral when she was buried in the same building in July 1587. She had been beheaded at Fotheringhay Castle in February that year but, mainly because of Queen Elizabeth's guilt over her rival's death, permission to bury the body in English soil was delayed for six months. Although it had been preserved in waxed winding-sheets the body was in a state of decomposition by hot July and the funeral had to be hastily arranged. As Peterborough was the nearest religious building of importance it was decided that the queen should be buried there. It is believed by some historians that her body was not actually in the coffin followed by all her mourners in 31st July but that it had been buried secretly the night before so that the smell did not offend so many noble people. The story is marvellously told in a long poem by the poet Alfred Noyes, called *The Burial of a Queen* which you will find in his book *Tales of the Mermaid Tavern*.

Mary Queen of Scots was, then, the second queen to be buried by Old Scarlett but her body remained in Peterborough Cathedral for only twenty-five years. In 1612 her son, King James I, moved his mother's body to Westminster Abbey. All that remains in Peterborough now are the queen's banners which still hang near the place where she was buried, on the opposite side of the sanctuary from Katharine of Aragon.

Old Scarlett buried one other important lady – at least for him. When his own wife Margaret died he buried her, not inside the cathedral but in the churchyard outside, where common people had their graves. The old grave-digger himself died in 1594 and now lies buried beneath his memorial stone just under the wall-painting.

Chapter Ten
THE COURAGEOUS DUTCHMAN?

Once again we have to return to that old problem of flooding and fen-drainage, and one of the most important characters in this part of our story is a Dutchman, named Cornelius Vermuyden.

Vermuyden was only twenty-six when he came to this country in 1621. As an engineer he was unrivalled and had already made quite a reputation for himself in Holland. King Charles invited him over to drain the Thames Marches near Dagenham, then the Great Park at Windsor and the Royal Chase at Hatfield in Yorkshire.

He was faced with many problems wherever he worked. He had difficulties with the English labourers, resentment from the local families in each area, and finally had to import Dutch workers over to complete each contract. Eventually he was able to report to the king that the work had been satisfactorily carried out and that 'all was well'. As a reward he was knighted on 6th January, 1629 and became Sir Cornelius Vermuyden at the age of thirty-four.

Then the king decided that it was time to start draining the Fens and adding more valuable land to his kingdom. But first of all he needed some sponsors, or backers, and so Charles I set up a committee under the chairmanship of Frances, Fourth Earl of Bedford, one of the country's most influential land-owners. This committee became known as The Gentlemen Adventurers because the people who formed it 'adventured' or risked their money in the scheme.

An agreement, known as the Lynn Law, was drawn up by which the Earl was to receive 95,000 acres, the rents from 40,000 to be spent on maintaining the works, and the Crown was to receive 12,000 acres. This may seem a modest share for the king but we must remember that he was gaining thousands of acres for his kingdom and even the rich could be taxed and made to pay more rent.

With their plans ready The Gentlemen Adventurers then announced that Cornelius Vermuyden was to be the engineer in charge of the operations. It was not a popular choice. Most of the Fenmen of that time did not want their land drained anyway and were quite content with conditions as they were. The Fens provided them with good fishing, plenty of wild-fowling, and good reeds for

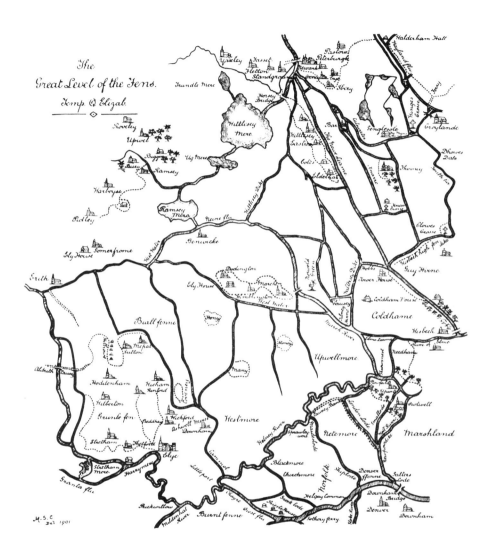

Map of Great Level of the Fens.

thatching their houses. They felt they could make an adequate living out of those boggy marshlands and they were seldom bothered by the Law. Why should they give up their rights and their independence just to satisfy the greedy king! When they heard that a foreigner had been put in charge they were furious and swore that they would never help him to complete his task. On the contrary, they were so hostile to his plans that they threatened they would destroy the work as fast as it was completed.

Once again the Dutch engineer had to rely on imported labour. It was a colossal problem from the word go. Not only was he short of men but he was also short of tools. In those days there was no sophisticated machinery, no dredgers or drag-lines, no pumps or bulldozers. Everything had to be done by hand, by pick and shovel. Even the strongest men found that they could not stand the long working hours in such awful conditions.

The work made slow progress and cost more money than was estimated. Some of the backers were financially ruined by the scheme and began to accuse Vermuyden of exploiting them. To make matters worse the weather also seemed determined to make the Dutchman give up his attempts at draining the Fens. Wet summers and long wet winters meant that there was more floodwater than usual and it was impossible to dig canals through such water-logged land.

Vermuyden's first plan had been an ambitious and daring one. Rather like Bishop Morton he could see that the winding rivers would never cope with so much water and that his most urgent task was to cut long straight drains from where the rivers entered the Fens so that the water could flow as quickly as possible out to sea.

One of the first excavations was a twenty-one mile long drain from Earith to Denver, almost as straight as a billiard-cue, and all dug by hand. In this way he was able to divert the unruly waters of the Great Ouse from their wayward course and direct them into a controlled relief-channel towards King's Lynn and The Wash. This drain became known as The Old Bedford River, after the Fourth Earl of Bedford who was the chief sponsor of The Gentlemen Adventurers.

It was called The *Old* Bedford River because Vermuyden's first plans did not quite work out as he'd expected and it was soon apparent that the drain was not adequate for the amount of water it had to take. So another and larger drain had to be cut, parallel with the first, and this became known as The *New* Bedford River. Both can still be seen today and are important historical as well as geographical landmarks in the Fens. One of the most thrilling views of this work can be had from a train as it passes over the Welney Washlands on its way from March to Ely.

The failure of Vermuyden's scheme to drain the Fens and keep the fields dry for more than a few months each year made the Fenmen even more resentful. The new dykes and rivers were spoiling their fishing and the partially reclaimed land was still not dry enough for anything but a few lean cattle to graze on in summer. True to their word they sabotaged Vermuyden's work wherever they could. They rioted, they blew-up the new sluices, they broke down the new river-banks, they even attacked some of the workmen who were brought into the Fens to do the work which they would not do.

But the work continued and the sponsors lost more money as they tried to support the king and keep faith with Vermuyden. Eventually, in 1637, they were able to declare that the drainage of the Fens was complete. They were, to say the least, being a little optimistic. The scheme had certainly not been the success which many people had hoped for and more than one of the backers ended up bankrupt.

So, rather like we did with Hereward the Wake, we have to ask the question 'Was Cornelius Vermuyden a hero or villain?' Some historians believe that the whole idea of Vermuyden's was wrong and that his drainage scheme was disastrous. Others, while admitting that he made mistakes, believe that he did the best that could have been done under the circumstances.

A 'banker' from plan of Wisbech new river, 1636.

Chapter Eleven
A CHAPTER OF DISASTERS

We cannot leave the subject of fen-drainage yet for there were to be several more dramatic moments during the lifetime of Vermuyden and his work was far from over. The declaration that the Fens had been successfully drained proved to be premature, for just a year later the floods returned with a vengeance.

Not only was Sir Cornelius Vermuyden bitterly disappointed, so too was Charles I. He had desperately wanted the scheme to be successful during his reign and even dreamt of building a great new palace near Manea – which he was going to re-name 'Charlemont'. The King thought it would be an ideal place to get away from the growing troubles in London and the increasing discontent of Parliament.

To make sure that the draining operations continued King Charles appointed himself as the Chairman of the New Gentlemen Adventurers and found more backers to provide the money. Vermuyden was kept on as the chief engineer but he was warned that this time his plans had better work.

It was not long before the King realised that he had greater problems than just draining the Fens. Many Members of Parliament were dissatisfied with him as their royal leader. They resented his firm belief in the Divine Right of Kings to rule, they objected to the way he raised taxes without their consent, and were not happy with his marriage to a Catholic princess, which they thought was disloyal to the Protestant cause.

The King demonstrated his power by having some of these politicians imprisoned without trial and by forming his own army, which he unwisely sent to raid the Houses of Parliament. The quarrels between the Government and the Crown became even more bitter and Civil War seemed inevitable. Although John Pym was one of the chief opponents of the King it was eventually left to a man from the Fens to claim attention in this troubled chapter of our history. His name was Oliver Cromwell, a farmer and landowner who was born at Huntingdon in 1599.

To begin with Cromwell was reluctant to become the leader of the Parliamentarians, but, as the disputes grew worse and the battles between the two sides more disorganised, it was clear that a strong

Oliver Cromwell, etched by P. S. Lamborn from an original by Samuel Cooper.

leader was needed. The full story of the Civil War needs a whole book to itself and many volumes on the subject have been written. We need only consider an outline of the main events to see them as part of the Fen-country's own development.

The Civil War began in 1642. By 1644 Cromwell's army had already won several decisive battles and these were followed by the famous victories at Marston Moor and Naseby. In 1646 the King decided to surrender himself to the Scots, who immediately handed him over to the English troops fighting for Cromwell. Three years later the Royalist cause was all over and Charles I was executed on 30th January, 1649.

The country was now without a monarch, without a properly elected Parliament, and in the hands of a dictator – a man who was known to despise Catholics and who showed no mercy to anyone who opposed him. To most people Cromwell soon came to be seen as a tyrant who ruled by terror. His army was one of the most efficient fighting forces in Europe, perhaps the first army to be so well-trained and disciplined since the Romans.

While all this fighting was going on Vermuyden and his men were still trying to drain the Fens, this time under the Chairmanship of William, the Fifth Earl of Bedford. The Great Bedford Level (the main area of land being drained) was divided into three sections – North Level, Middle Level and South Level. The second drain was cut from Earith to Denver which (as we saw in the last chapter) was called the New Bedford River, or the One Hundred Foot Drain. It was one hundred feet wide and twenty-one miles long and was meant to take all the excess floodwater of the Great Ouse.

Several other drains were also cut through the Fens, many of them with unromantic names like Forty Foot and Twenty Foot. Some were even named after a few of Cromwell's supporters and one was called Paupers' Cut because the work was done by men who were living on the Parish Poor Rates, which was a bit like being on the dole today. In those days people had to do some kind of work to earn the Parish money, even if they were old and could do no more than fill up holes in the roads with stones.

Most of the heavy labouring-work in the draining of the Fens was now being done by a thousand Scottish prisoners-of-war who had been captured at the battle of Dunbar. Later, Vermuyden had to enlarge his work force by using five hundred Dutch prisoners who had been taken in the naval battle between Admiral Blake and Admiral van Tromp. There was a touch of irony in the situation of a Dutchman working for the English employing Dutch prisoners of war who had been fighting the English.

All these prisoners – both Scottish and Dutch – had to face the anger and hostility of the local Fenmen who were still opposed to the idea of draining their land. In addition to these hazards, the prisoners had to contend with the dreadfully damp climate and began to suffer with the fen ague. Several of them died and others, it is believed, were actually murdered by local gangs known as 'wreckers'.

In spite of all these troubles Vermuyden's work slowly progressed and the shape and nature of the Fens were changed for all time by people who had little interest in the Fen-country. Some, it is true, decided to settle down in the area, marry local girls and make their home here, but for many it was a time of misery.

At last, on 25th March, 1652, Vermuyden was able to say that the task of draining the Fens was now complete. A week later a Service of Thanksgiving was held in Ely Cathedral for which special anthems were composed and prayers written. At this point the battle with the water appeared to have been won and Sir Cornelius Vermuyden retired from the scene to live the rest of his life in seclusion in London, where he died in October 1677 at the age of eighty-two.

But the story of the floods did not end there. Less than thirty years later the countryside was again under water. After several prolonged wet winters the land was wetter than it had been for a long time and the dykes could not contain the additional water coming down from the uplands of Bedfordshire, Northampton and Lincolnshire.

Although much of Vermuyden's work had, in the end, been successful as far as he was concerned, it had created other problems. Draining the land was, as described earlier, like squeezing the water out of a bath-sponge. It grew smaller. The soft peat soil of the black Fens started to shrink and dry out. As the land shrank so it naturally became lower. That meant it was even more difficult to get the water up into the rivers and out to the Wash.

The solution to this problem introduced a new landmark to dominate the Fenland skyline – the windmill.

Forty Foot Drain.

Picture courtesy of John Baguley.

Chapter Twelve
HARNESSING THE WIND AND STEAM

These Fens *have oft times been by* Water *drown'd*
Science a remedy in Water *found*
The power of Steam *she said shall be employ'd*
And the Destroyer *by* Itself *destroy'd.*

Plaque on the Hundred Foot Engine, 1830.

If today, you were to take an aerial view of the Fens, the picture would reveal a vast network of dykes, rivers and roads dissecting the fields until the countryside looks more like a giant chessboard.

On the other hand, if you simply travelled at ground level you would notice that many of those waterways are now much higher than the roads themselves. This was one of the main problems facing the drainage engineers who followed Vermuyden.

A large area of Fenland is below sea-level, making it a kind of shallow basin – a hollow. Because water will not flow uphill without mechanical means it has to be lifted, stage by stage, from the lower land to the higher, until it can be pumped into the rivers which will eventually take it out to sea.

In the seventeenth and eighteenth centuries this was done mainly by windmills – a system which had already proved successful in Holland. The mills used for drainage were not as large as the mills used for grinding corn but they did have sails and most visitors to the area thought them picturesque. At one time there were a thousand of them lining the dykesides throughout the Fens.

The mills had the usual long sails for catching the wind and very large scoop-wheels for scooping up the water. Sometimes these were inside the mill, sometimes outside. As the wind turned the sails, the shaft inside the mill turned the wheel which lifted the water from one level to the other. In this way the water in the dykes which could not flow up to the higher river levels was raised mechanically into the main outlets and helped on its way to the sea.

But, of course, windmills depend on the wind and unless the wind blows the sail won't go round. And if the sails do not go round then the scoop-wheel remains useless and the water in the dykes cannot get away. Even when the wind did blow it did not always blow in the right direction, so the mills still did not work. Eventually some of the more sophisticated ones were built so that they could be

Drainage mill and wheel near Boston.

swivelled round to catch the wind, but this was not easy and men could not be employed just for that purpose. Often they were called from the fields to haul the mill round to catch the wind and then went back to their daily job. There was also the problem of too much wind. If a gale was blowing, the sails had to be anchored down, otherwise they and the scoop-wheels would have gone spinning crazily round causing even more havoc. There was another problem in winter when the dykes (and sometimes the rivers) froze so that the mills again stood idle.

It was all a laborious, hit-and-miss affair. Although attractive to look at, the windmill was not always successful at doing the job for which it was built. But even when it became obsolete there were many people who were sad to see its days come to an end. We can see from old prints and pictures that windmills did add their own kind of beauty to the landscape. Apart from churches they were the only vertical shapes on the skyline.

But if the Fens were ever to be drained properly the drainage engineers needed something that was more than just attractive. They wanted a mill that was efficient, something they could control.

Fortunately, the industrial revolution of the nineteenth century was beginning to produce machinery which did not rely on the chance of wind and water. The age of steam had arrived, and with it the steam-engine. It was not long before this new power was brought to the Fens and, by 1820, the age of the windmill was over. Pumping stations with tall chimneys took the place of mills with sails and were to stay for a hundred years. Some of them can still be seen today along the sides of rivers or dykes but they too are now obsolete and mostly stand in ruins.

Of the ones which are left the best example of what a steam pumping-house looked like is at Stretham, near Ely, which is well worth a visit. It was one of the last pumping stations to be operated by steam and was kept in use until 1947 when it did a magnificent job of trying to control the disastrous floods of that year.

But even the age of steam was to come to an end. Diesel engines took the place of steam-engines and, from 1950 onwards, electrical motors became the main source of driving power for the modern pumping stations.

However sophisticated the machinery, keeping the Fens dry is always a constant battle which people long after us will have to continue. In this century alone the upland waters and sea have combined to threaten the lives of all who live in the Fens. 1936, 1937, 1939, 1947 and 1953 are some of the dates which Fen-people remember very clearly. The same tragedies have happened to them as happened to families who lived two, three or four hundred years ago. Their homes have been washed away, their cattle drowned, even their children lost in the cruel floods.

In this constant battle with water more than a handful of names deserve to be mentioned. It did not all start or end with Sir Cornelius Vermuyden. Famous engineers such as Thomas Telford, Charles and Nathanial Kinderley, and John Rennie, all made important contributions to Fen-drainage.

Stretham Pump House.   *Picture courtesy of John Baguley.*

Chapter Thirteen
THE MOCKING WIND

Before we leave the unending problem of Fen-drainage there is one more aspect of it we must consider – the shrinking of the land once it is drained. Some areas of the Fens are now six-and-a-half metres lower than they were in 1850. As well as the land shrinking it also gets very dry, like dust, and when strong winds blow – especially in the spring when the new seed has just been sown – the outcome can be devastating. These winds which whip off the top soil and carry it away are called *Fen Blows*.

Fen Blows are a natural event which we can do little about. It would be rather like trying to stop a sandstorm in a desert. Because the Fens are so open and flat there is nothing to deter the force or direction of the wind. The land is very exposed, there are few trees, no hills or natural wind-breaks. When a gale-force wind wants to blow across the Fens it advances like a victorious army over a battlefield. Modern farming methods have gone some way towards protecting the newly-planted seeds but all too often on such days the farmer can only watch helplessly as the wind attacks his land.

The majority of Fen soil is peat, that is decayed vegetation, which quickly reduces in size when moisture is taken from it, particularly at surface level where the wind hastens the drying process. When this happens the soil becomes very light and powdery and easily gets blown away, sometimes for miles.

Fen Blows are particularly dangerous in spring when fields have just been drilled with sugar-beet and the seed has begun to germinate. The wind whips up the fine soil into a huge cloud of dust and blows it high into the sky, very often as far as the next village. Much of the newly-planted seed goes with it, to fall on someone else's land, and the farmer is forced to drill his fields for a second or third time.

Some farmers have planted rows of trees to reduce the force of the wind on their crops but this is only partially successful. Until recent years farmers were more likely to pull down their trees to make better use of the land. It is possible now to grow crops of weeds on the land before planting the sugar-beet seed and this helps to knit the top-soil together, giving the seed a better chance. The weeds (which some people call a 'nurse crop') are then burnt off with a spray, once the seedlings are established. Other farmers plant straw in between the rows of beet and this eventually rots away or can be ploughed out when the crop is well on the way. Seed can also be grown in capsule form which gives it more hope of surviving. But a Fen Blow is still something that Fen people fear and you will not see anything like it anywhere else in England.

It can be a terrifying and awesome experience with clouds of dust travelling above you, darkening the sky so that it is necessary to have car headlights on even at midday. Familiar roads disappear or get strewn with pieces of hedgerow and tree. People in the path of a Fen Blow seal their doors and windows with sticky tape, and still the fine dust gets in to cover furniture and crockery.

Perhaps the most remarkable example of how much the soil has shrunk in the Fens during the last hundred years or more, can be seen at Holme Fen, near Yaxley. When it was decided in 1849 to drain Whittlesey Mere there was considerable concern among some of the engineers that this would result in the surrounding land shrinking at an alarming rate. To prove their point a cast-iron post, which had come from the Great Exhibition in London (1851), was driven like a nail into the soil until its top was at ground level. Those landowners who wanted the Mere drained thought they had seen the last of the post. But the engineers were right. Slowly the land at Holme Fen started to shrink and the post began to emerge like something left by a receding tide. By 1963 it was so exposed that it had to be supplemented by a new post on a concrete base close-by, which has gone on recording the shrinking of the land right up to this day. Holme Fen Post now registers that the ground-level is more than six metres lower than it was when the post was first driven into the soil. A notice fixed to the post says that you can even feel the soil tremble.

As you travel about the Fens other examples of soil shrinkage caused by drainage can be found, such as houses on the tilt, leaning over, or hunched as if their backs are broken, some with extra doorsteps added to them so that people can reach their front doors.

Roads suffer in the same way. As the land beneath them is always on the move they gradually turn into switchbacks. Roads can be flattened out and resurfaced but a year later the bumps and hollows are back as the land subsides again.

Because there is always a conflict with nature in the Fens there is

Dust storm in the black fens. Welches Dam, Isle of Ely, April 4th, 1949.

Picture courtesy of Wisbech Advertiser.

also always a sense of adventure. The mocking wind can scare the living daylight out of you as it hurls those great clouds of dust across the land during a Fen Blow but it can just as easily excite as it pushes gigantic layers of cloud like ice-bergs across the sky. People can get angry about the wind as it batters their houses but they can also joke about it. As one man said to me a few years ago 'This is the only part of England where you can see two people biking against a head wind, both going in opposite directions'. Another source of excitement is to travel along some of those Fen roads which run parallel to a main river. Because the land has shrunk the road can be several metres lower than the level of the water held within the banks. It's not a very comforting thought on a stormy day to realise that if those banks burst you would be swept away by millions of gallons of water flowing well above your head.

River banks are marvellous places from which to get a good view of the Fens. On a bright day you can see for thirty miles or more away. You look over what John Clare the poet called 'a many-coloured atlas' and if you belong to the Fens you feel a certain pride in knowing that that vast fertile world before you is largely the work of Man.

Effect of soil shrinkage, ground level was originally on the level of the top step.

Picture courtesy of John Baguley.

Chapter Fourteen
RIOTS IN THE FENS

Most of us today can take our food for granted. We know where the next meal is coming from and can look forward to our favourite pizza or fish-and-chips with certainty. But there are many older people in the Fens who can look back to a childhood when meat was a luxury and vegetables were eked out by using wild plants from the fields and hedgerows. For them a sheep's head was a banquet and had to provide the basis of several meals to come, until the bones were as bare as pebbles on a beach. Some can remember their parents talking about those days when there was no food at all and no chance of earning any money with which to buy food because there was no work on the land.

Just over a hundred years ago so many country people were out of work and hungry that they decided to leave England altogether and try their luck in some of the new colonies. During what we call 'the agricultural depression' of the nineteenth century over half a million farm-labourers left this country for Australia, New Zealand and Canada. Many others, who were expert craftsmen of their time, had to take to the roads as beggars, or went into other jobs in order to satisfy their families' hunger.

One of the worst periods of social unrest in the Fens came during the early 1800's, a period of depression aggravated by the long drawn-out Napoleonic Wars with France. As so often happens during such troubled times people became desperate and were prepared to take the law into their own hands. As one of the Littleport rioters said in 1816 'I might as well be hanged as starve'.

Although there had been a number of uprisings in the Fens, at places like Upware, Southery and Downham, the most notorious took place in Littleport. On 22nd May, 1816, a group of Littleport men met at The Globe public-house for their annual Benefit Club Meeting to see which families most urgently needed help. It was soon clear that everyone was in need of food and money. It was also plain to see that most of the men were discontented and angry. Those who could find work were forced to accept wages of about 40p a week. That did not even allow them enough to buy bread for their families because the price of wheat had risen to what would be the equivalent of £500–£600 today, making flour impossible to buy for the poor. Wives and mothers boiled nettles for soup and toasted the last stale crusts of bread until it was black, then they crumbled it into a powder, added some pepper and boiling water so that it resembled tea.

Against this background of poverty and hardship it was understandable that the talk in the Globe public-house turned to rebellion. The men had heard that farm-workers in other parts of the Fens were 'kicking up a fuss' and demanding more money to keep their families alive. Some of the Littleport men had already spent their Benefit money on too much beer and were slightly drunk. They decided it was time to teach some of the wealthier people of the town a lesson. One of the local farmers and magistrates was known to spend more on one new shirt than he would on the wages of three men he had just sacked. He was soon put to the top of the 'hit list' with several other tradespeople joining him.

Arming themselves with whatever home-made weapons they could find – clubs, forks, cudgels and cleavers, they set off into the dark streets and began to ransack property and threaten innocent people. Furniture was hacked to pieces and food stolen from pantries. When Josiah Dewey, a retired farmer, refused to give the rioters £1 they forced their way into his house, cleared the rooms of linen, clocks, cutlery and china, then went on to the next victim. When they approached the vicar's house he threatened to shoot the first man who put a foot on his land. But the mob surged into the vicarage, rampaged through the library and were so busy smashing up the house that they did not notice the vicar and his family escape to Ely where they woke up two other magistrates – the Reverend William Metcalfe and Reverend Sir Henry Bate Dudley.

Having caused as much damage in Littleport as they could the rioters then reassembled at The Globe to make plans for an attack on Ely. They had collected a better arsenal of weapons from their raids on local houses and had both fire-arms and ammunition. They stole a farm cart and on it mounted four punt guns. These long barrelled guns were usually used by fowlers out on the marshes and, with a pound of shot, could kill at a distance of a hundred metres. In the early hours of the morning the rebels marched off to Ely.

In the meantime the Ely magistrates had sent a messenger to

Bury St Edmunds for troop reinforcements from the garrison there. So, while the Littleport men were making their way to the Market Place in Ely, soldiers from the Royal Dragoons and Royston Volunteer Cavalry were approaching from the opposite direction. The rioters arrived in the city first and demanded to see the local magistrates who were now meeting in The White Hart Inn. Mr Metcalfe, speaking from one of the windows, asked the men what they wanted. 'Give us the price of a stone of flour a day' shouted some of the men, 'or twopence for a pint of beer' shouted some of the more rowdy. 'Our children are starving. We want a living wage!'

The magistrates retired for further discussion and then issued the following statement: 'The Magistrates agree, and do order, that the over-seers shall pay to each family Two shillings per Head per Week, when Flour is Half-a-crown a stone; such allowance to be raised in proportion when the price of flour is higher, and that the price of labour shall be Two Shilling a day, whether married or single and that the labourer shall be paid his full wages by the Farmer who hires him'.

The Agreement seemed fair and was accepted by the men who were then stupidly given free beer by the relieved magistrates and told to go home. Many of the Littleport men with genuine grievances kept their part of the bargain and returned to their families but a lot of the hangers-on accepted the drinks and started celebrating noisily in the streets. At that point the soldiers arrived and the celebrations turned into warfare. During the next two days more than eighty prisoners were taken and one man – Thomas Sindall – was shot.

A Special Court was set up and the prisoners brought in for trial. Judge Abbot listened to each case and concluded that the men's action had not in any way been caused by distress or hunger but by lawlessness. He then sentenced twenty-four of the prisoners (including one woman, Sarah Hobbs) to death and named those who were to be transported to Botany Bay for periods of seven to fourteen years. The less guilty were to be jailed in Ely.

These harsh sentences caused an outcry in Ely and Littleport and those people who had been prepared to accept the magistrates' conditions now rallied to the support of the men who had been caught. Had the streets not still been full of armed soldiers there would have been more violence and rioting. The seething resent-

ment among the people finally forced the Judge to reconsider the sentences he had passed for fear of his own life. Of the twenty-four who were to hang, nineteen were reprieved and sent to Botany Bay for life, a decision which some thought no better than swinging from a rope.

The five who did not get a reprieve were William Beamiss, George Crow, John Dennis, Isaac Harley and Thomas South. They went to the gallows on Friday, 28th June and a crowd of several hundred arrived to see this tragic end to a tragic chapter of Fenland history. The bodies of the hanged men were later buried together in the churchyard of St Mary's, Ely.

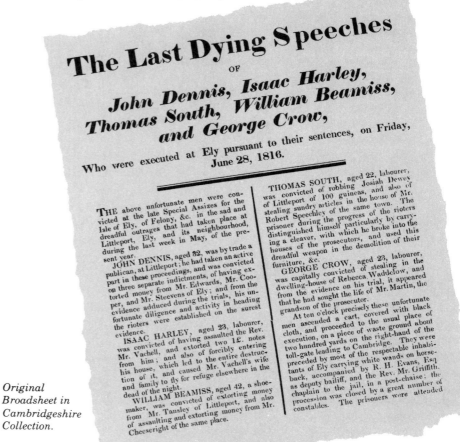

Original Broadsheet in Cambridgeshire Collection.

Chapter Fifteen
THE LAST OF THE MERES

After that last chapter of drama and turmoil we return to a quieter event which also caused a great deal of interest among Fen people – the draining of Whittlesey Mere.

This great expanse of water was not a big, dull, uninteresting puddle, it was more like a lake, with an attractive shore-line and jetties, and was often used for regattas – or water-picnics as they were sometimes called.

The poet John Clare used to walk all the way from his home in Helpston to Whittlesey Mere just to admire the many species of ferns. On 25th March, 1825, he wrote to his friend Mr Henderson of Milton Hall: *'We have many famous ferns. There is a beautiful one called 'Lady Fern' growing among the boggy spots of Whittlesea Mere and a dwarf willow grows there about a foot high, which it never exceeds. It is also a place very common for the cranberry that trails by the brink of the Mere. There are several waterweeds too with very beautiful or peculiar flowers . . .'.*

There we have a first-hand account of how attractive the Mere must have been. It was also the habitat of the swallow-tail butterfly, rare moths, birds, golden-ringed snakes, zebra-spiders and exotic flowers, none of which can be found in Fens today.

In the seventeenth century water-picnics on the Mere were very popular and William Pierrepont of Orton arranged one to entertain the Bishop of Peterborough and his clergy. It was an extravagant affair which began with melons and port wine. Then came venison, pasties, rounds of beef, legs and shoulders of mutton, ducks and

Regatta on Whittlesey Mere from a drawing by J. M. Heathcote, 1876.

chickens, apples, cakes and tarts, and more wine.

On public holidays people used to gather at the Mere as they would at an Agricultural Show, gymkhana or fairground. All round the shores of the Mere would be side-shows, amusements, stalls and tradesmen, You could have bought hot chestnuts, sausages, pork-pies, doughnuts and cakes. There was even a bandstand where a group of musicians provided just the right kind of joyful music for such an occasion.

The Mere did have its darker side and was well-known for getting very stormy in bad weather. Some of the storms were quite unpredictable and appeared to have nothing to do with the weather at all. People called these storms 'water-quakes' because they were like earth-quakes rising up from the bed of the Mere. Several wrecks of sunken boats were discovered in the mud when the Mere was drained.

In the eighteenth century the wealthy Lord Orford set sail with a fleet of nine small sailing ships to travel through 'the narrow seas of Cambridgeshire, Lincolnshire, Huntingdonshire, Norfolk and Suf-

Drainage of Whittlesey Mere – the dyke cutting.

Illustrated London News.

44

folk'. He too experienced one of the Mere's freak storms and in his log-book entry for 26th July, 1774, wrote that early in the morning 'the wind was blowing hard' and that the boats knocking into each other 'alarmed the sleeping crew, who thought they were being driven on to some hidden rocks'. Some of the ladies were sea-sick and frightened. But, by nine o'clock that morning, the Mere was 'quite calm again and the water as smooth as a looking-glass'.

So, when we consider how much the Mere was used and enjoyed by people for their pleasure and what excellent fishing it provided, we can understand why there was so much resentment to the plans for draining it; although it must be said that the Mere was getting so shallow with all the other drainage going on around it, that its natural life would soon have been over anyway.

The drainage of the Mere was at last made possible in the nineteenth century by the new invention of a pump engine known as 'the Appold Centrifugal Pump', which was demonstrated at the Great Exhibition of 1851. This remarkable piece of equipment could pump out water at the rate of 1,680 gallons a minute and was immediately engaged to drain Whittlesea Mere.

It was still a huge task, equivalent to draining something the size of Hickling Broad or Lake Derwentwater. Whittlesea Mere also varied in size and volume of water depending on the seasons. In winter it covered more than 3,000 acres; in summer it was often reduced to 1,700 acres.

People came from miles around to witness the disappearance of what was then the last largest natural 'lake' in Southern England. they came with home-made trucks, push-carts, old prams and buckets, to grab what they could from the bed of the dying Mere. They caught hundreds of tons of fish which were left gasping in the shallow waters – roach, perch, chubb, bream, pike and eels. Even then, thousands of fish were left to die and rot.

What was more interesting as the Mere dried out was the collection of relics found just below the mud – the skulls of wild boar, a wolf, a whale and a prehistoric canoe cut out of oak. Equally interesting were a silver incense-boat, a silver censer and silver chandelier which had once belonged to Ramsey Abbey. These must have been thrown overboard by monks escaping from Ramsey at the time of the Dissolution of the Monasteries in the fifteenth century, or perhaps their boat capsized in one of the Mere's freak storms.

On the day that the Mere was drained more than the water disappeared. Two thousand years of history went with it and that great area is now rich farmland, growing wheat, barley, potatoes and sugar-beet.

If you visit the site of Whittlesey Mere with a copy of a modern Ordnance Survey Map and a copy of Bodger's Map of 1786 (see inside back cover) you will still be able to trace the shoreline and landing-stages which were once so popular two hundred years ago.

Ancient boat found in Whittlesey Mere.

Chapter Sixteen
SKATING IN THE FENS

One of the pastimes on Whittlesey Mere which I did not mention was ice-skating, but that was a sport enjoyed throughout the Fens whenever there was a stretch of water which could be frozen in winter. It still is, but not to the extent it was seventy or eighty years ago, mainly because we do not get the great expanses of floodwater now, nor do we seem to get such long hard winters as the old Fenmen can remember.

Half a century ago a hard winter could easily put two or three thousand farm-labourers out of work for several weeks. If it was going to be a long winter they hoped it would be a hard frosty one, rather than wet, because with plenty of frosts they knew there would be plenty of ice. And, if you had nothing else better to do, why not spend a few days skating?

Such winters and such vast areas of ice were largely responsible for producing the great Fen skaters, some of whom became national champions and legends in their own lifetime – men like Turkey Smart, Fish Smart, James Smart, Gutta Percha See, Charles Tebutt, the Staples brothers and the Slaters, the Smiths and the Drakes, all earned a reputation for themselves equal to today's footballers and snooker-players.

In 1895, Charles Tebbutt completed a trip of 83 miles in nine hours. But it was not distance that mattered so much as speed. Skaters who went in for racing could reach fifteen to twenty miles an hour. It was not uncommon to skate thirty or forty miles a day and people frequently found that skates were the only form of transport from one place to another in a severe winter.

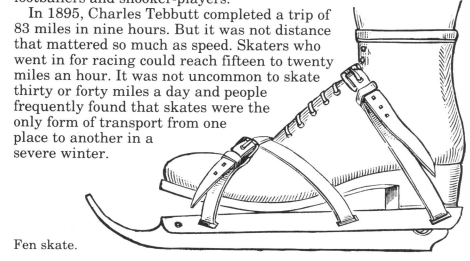

Fen skate.

Fenland skater.

STATISTICS.

National Skating Association, established to promote Speed, *March 1, 1879.*
" " extended to promote Figure Skating, *Dec. 30, 1880.*

ASSOCIATION RACE MEETINGS, 1879—80.

FIRST CHAMPIONSHIP MEETING (Thorney), *Dec. 8, 1879.*

One Mile and-a-Half, with six turns. Ice bad through Snow. Official time taken by Mr J. D. Digby.

FIRST ROUND.

J. Nichols, Peterborough	beat J. Wignell, Asfordby	60 yds.	7 m. 15 s.
N. Brown, Isleham	" E. Smith, Whittlesea	Fell.	7 m. 7 s.
Jarmin Smart, Welney	" W. Rich, Harrow	Easily.	6 m. 32 2/5 s.
J. Walpole, Tyd Gote	" F. W. Coles, Peterborough	50 yds.	6 m. 16 4/5 s.
G. Smart, Welney	" W. Howitt, Wisbech	Easily.	6 m. 2 s.
J. Neaverson, Peakirk	" R. Naylor, Upwell	5 yds.	6 m. 14 2/5 s.
J. Collin, Soham Fen	" S. Mole, Wisbech	40 yds.	6 m. 45 3/5 s.
A. Dewsberry, Oxlode	" A. Palmer, Barway	100 yds.	6 m. 29 s.
J. Pickering, Cowbit	" J. Brown, Isleham	12 yds.	Stpd. prematurely.
L. Register, Southery, skated a bye	" A. Houblon, Aylesbury, absent.		
W. Collison, Nottingham	beat W. Johnson, Little Downham	80 yds.	6 m. 43 2/5 s.
J. Brown, Southery	" Turkey Smart, Welney	20 yds.	6 m. 28 s.
G. See, Welney	" B. T. Birch, Lynn	150 yds.	6 m. 26 2/5 s.
T. Watkinson, Upwell	" A. H. Hawes, Welney	50 yds.	6 m. 6 s.
H. Carter, Welney	" H. Williams, Boro' Fen	100 yds.	6 m. 20 s.

SECOND ROUND.

N. Brown	beat Nichols	50 yds.	6 m. 25 2/5 s.
Jarmin Smart	" Walpole	50 yds.	5 m. 56 2/5 s.
G. Smart	" Neaverson	100 yds.	
Dewsberry	" Collin	50 yds.	6 m. 56 s.
Pickering	" Register	4 yds.	6 m. 43 2/5 s.
Brown	" Collison	12 yds.	6 m. 30 s.
Watkinson	" See	50 yds.	6 m. 14 s.
Carter skated a bye.			

THIRD ROUND.

J. Smart	beat N. Brown	Easily.	
G. Smart	" Dewsberry	Eased up, 6 m. 4 1/6 s.	
J. Brown	" Pickering	Easily.	
Carter	" Watkinson	40 or 50 yds.	

FOURTH ROUND.

G. Smart	beat J. Smart	20 yds.	6 m. 18 s.
Carter	" Brown	100 yds.	

DECIDING COURSE.

G. Smart beat H. Carter, and became the First Champion of England. Won by 20 yds. The last race was run almost in the dark and with a great deal of water on the ice.

During the eighty years that bridged the turn of the century there were some great skating scenes in the Fens. The ice would be as crowded as a carnival field. But it was not always skating for fun. Many of the men entered the races to win food for their families – a side of bacon, a pig's head, a leg of mutton, loaves of bread, or pork pies. Such competitions became known as the 'Bread and Meat' Races, and many children were kept from hunger by the skill and speed of their fathers on skates.

You can still see old prints in museums and libraries of these Fenland scenes, with the skaters bent nearly double to cut down wind-resistance, one arm behind the back, the other working like a piston to build up the speed.

Skating had been popular in England since the twelfth century. When the River Thames was frozen, Londoners used a primitive form of skate made of sheep's leg-bones. Several hundred years later, in the winter of 1662, Samuel Pepys – the famous diarist – wrote that he had been to watch the gentlemen 'skating in Hyde Park'.

Skating was also a popular sport in countries such as Holland and Norway and eventually the Norwegian skates, already fixed to the boots, were to replace the old Fenland 'runners' which were no more than blades made by the local blacksmith and then fastened to ordinary boots by straps and screws.

My own grandfather used to make a little extra money at the skating-matches by hiring out a wooden chair so that the skaters could sit down and fix on their skates. He then made another penny or two by helping to sweep the Course for the racers.

I can remember spending days out on the flooded washlands at Whittlesey when I was a boy of eight or nine. Older boys often stayed out until it got dark and then skated in the moonlight. Our local fish-and-chip van would also be out there on the ice, frying for ten hours a day, like an old tramp-steamer marooned in that frozen sea, its narrow drain-pipe chimney oozing with black smoke against an arctic sky.

Although the great skating days and the great skating names are past, you can still see something of what it was like out at Cowbit, Welney, Mepal and Bury – *if* we get some floods and hard frosts to make it possible.

Chapter Seventeen
A MEMORABLE BATTLE

Before moving on, we still need one more chapter on the subject of floods in order to tell of an event which many older people still remember, one of the most dramatic battles ever fought against the old scourge – water.

It took place in the spring of 1947, when most people were beginning to think that the worst of the winter was over and that they could now get on with the job of sowing the fields and growing their crops.

There had been a long winter with recent heavy falls of snow. Severe frosts had cracked the soils of the flood-banks, and a sudden thaw in the uplands created an enormous weight of water for the Fenland rivers to hold. The engineers were worried but believed that all the modern methods of draining the Fens would be

Building damaged by flood between Earith and Haddenham, March 1947.

Photo: Cambridgeshire Libraries.

adequate to cope with any crisis. They had powerful pumps, good channels. Providing that high tides did not make it impossible to use Denver Sluice they would be able to get all the surplus water away.

But that was not to be. High tides were forecast and March winds reached speeds of up to one hundred miles an hour. The alert went out – 'Strengthen the banks'. 'Start filling sand-bags for protection.' And the water began to rise. Soon it reached danger point.

By 13th March many of the roads around Earith and Welney were under water and virtually impassable. Floods were rising everywhere in the Fens at a frightening rate. The level of water in the Ouse was now twenty feet above the level of the surrounding land. If the banks burst disaster was imminent.

And still the wind howled across the Fens, bringing down trees and telegraph-poles so that communication between one town and another became impossible. In Ely, people began to evacuate their homes, or to raise their furniture on piles of bricks to clear the water now creeping into their houses. In some streets the water was knee-deep. The railway station at Littleport was closed, trains were stopped.

By Sunday evening, 16th March, news came through that the River Lark was about to burst its banks. Villagers in Burnt Fen were advised by the Police to leave their homes and seek refuge at the Mildenhall Air Base. Soldiers who were stationed in the area were brought in to help.

The Fen landscape was now beginning to look more like a muddy battlefield as Army vehicles, amphibious tanks, lighting equipment and men in uniforms filled the scene. Everyone's attention now was fixed on survival. Ordinary life had to be suspended as all hands turned to fighting the floods.

But the water was relentless and came pouring down from the uplands of Bedfordshire and Northamptonshire. The Great Ouse bursts its banks in two more places. The villages of Over and Willingham were quickly flooded as the water rushed down to Earith and the Old West River. More than two thousand acres of rich farmland was drowned.

One of the ironies of the disaster was that the rivers could not even be used for transport because the level of the water was now so high no boats or barges could pass under the bridges.

Straggling columns of homeless people could be seen making their way like refugees along what roads remained above water. They did not know whether they would ever see their homes again. Some slept in village halls, some in churches, others went to relatives on safer ground. And all around them spread that great sea of swirling muddy water.

By Monday evening the scene was one of total desolation. Only a few rooftops could be seen sticking through the muddy water, showing where the deserted houses now stood.

To co-ordinate all the rescue work a military headquarters was set up in the preparatory department of Ely High School, and the campaign was suitably nicknamed *OPERATION NOAH'S ARK*.

Aerial photographs taken at the time show just how extensive the floods were. The whole of the Fens were either under water or threatened by water. On Saturday, 22nd March, the dam in the culvert near Southery collapsed and all the hard work put in by the thousands of men involved in the battle was brushed aside as of little consequence. The violence of the newly released water ripped up the roads and poured in a torrent a quarter of a mile wide over the fields. The force of water was so great that it tore a solid, double-fronted house in half. The owner's belongings, which had been stored upstairs for safety, were swept away like matchsticks – easy chairs, a settee, tables and cupboards. He could only stand on the river-bank and watch in disbelief.

I have talked with men in the Prickwillow and Littleport areas who can remember what it was like. 'It wasn't only the water coming off the banks' said one, 'It seemed to be coming up from underneath the ground as well. I could see my garden rising up and down like that, pumping like a man's heart. That were frightening, I can tell you'.

The end of the house belonging to another man was blown out as though someone had put a high explosive charge under it and he lost all his belongings in twelve minutes.

But, such is the character of the Fen people, they fought back and, by the end of the month, the floods started to subside and men and women began the arduous task of rebuilding their homes. Even where the houses still stood they found all the windows broken and the floors inside deep in smelling mud. It took many weeks to dry out the rooms, to buy new carpets and furniture, to get back to a normal life.

Although those floods of 1947 are the ones which older people still talk about there have been others since which have again tested the character of the Fen people. In January 1953 the whole of East Anglia was threatened by some of the most disastrous sea-floods in living memory. Once again high tides and high winds combined to produce high levels of water in the rivers and dykes. Sea-walls were brushed aside by gigantic waves, river-banks burst yet again, and thousands of acres of rich farmland were back under water. But this time it was even more serious for the farmers because most of that water was salt-water and it took years for the land to recover.

There was more flooding in 1978, aggravated by gale-force winds which stripped houses of their roofs, tore down barns, and blocked roads with trees. Cars were swept away like Dinky toys and hundreds of animals perished before they could be reached.

Water has always been both enemy and friend of the Fenland people. We cannot be sure that similar tragedies will not happen again.

Flood water destroying a house on the Southery Road.

Chapter Eighteen
THE FENS TODAY

Today as we drive through this part of Britain we are able to look at the thousands of acres of potatoes, sugar-beet, wheat, oil-seed rape, carrots, celery, onions and (especially in the Lincolnshire fens) bulb crops such as tulips and daffodils, all growing where once there was only a wasteland. The old description of the Fen country as 'a low, boggy, marshy area of land unfit for cultivation' is no longer true. The Fens are now amongst the richest, most efficiently farmed land in Europe. And this success is the result of a lot of hard work from a great many people, people who have learnt how to adapt to history and change.

At the beginning of this century the fields were worked by gangs of labourers – men, women and children – who did all the pea-pulling, potato-lifting, beet-chopping and harvesting by hand.

Harvesting the fens.

Picture courtesy of John Baguley.

Working families lived on the farms and the hard work often made people old before their time. Today most of that work is done by machines and farm-workers have to be very skilled now in new techniques and expensive equipment. Not as many agricultural workers live on the farms today, they prefer their own houses (instead of the tied cottages which often went with the job) and travel to work in their own cars. Because of this some of the old rural customs and attitudes have changed. The farming community is not what it was and many of the older people feel that the 'spirit of the place' has gone forever.

But has it? Although we may sit and watch television and feel the whole world is at our doorstep, although we may go abroad for our holidays and belong to the Common Market, people are still part of the landscape they inherit, still part of the traditions and customs which somehow survive from generation to generation. There will always be Fen people so long as there are Fens.

Sadly, there are many subjects which this brief history has not had space to cover. Why, for instance, do we not see large herds of cattle or flocks of sheep in the Fens as we do in say, Yorkshire, Cumbria or Wales? Why have potatoes been grown in the Fens for a hundred and seventy years but sugar-beet has been grown only for just about sixty years? Why are carrots and celery such traditional Fenland crops, and why grow ten thousand acres of tulips just to pull their heads off, or set fire to corn-stubble at the end of the harvest?

The answers to these questions can be found in the more detailed history books on the area listed at the end of this book, just as there are much fuller accounts of some of the Wildlife Nature Reserves and protected Fens, such as those at Welney, Wicken, and Woodwalton.

Enough has been said, I hope, to send you out on your own adventures, to explore and enjoy those places which are part of the English countryside, part of English history, and part of your world now. As the writer H. M. Tomlinson once said 'Adventure is never anywhere unless we make it.'

Fen Sky.
Picture courtesy of John Baguley.

SELECTED BOOK LIST

ASTBURY, A. K. *The Black Fens* Golden Head Pr., 1958.

BARKER, Dudley. *Harvest home: the official story of the great floods of 1947 and their sequel.* New ed. Providence Press, 1985.

BARRETT, W. H. *More tales from the Fens.* Routledge & K.P., 1964.

BARRETT, W. H. *Tales from the Fens.* Routledge & K.P., 1963.

BARRETT, W. H. *Battle of the banks.* Ely Rotary Club, 1947 (reprinted Cambridgeshire Libraries).

BECKETT, J. G. A. *Urgent hour: drainage of the Burnt Fen District in the South Level of the Fens, 1760–1981.* EARO, 1983.

BEVIS, Trevor A. *Churches of marsh and fen and their environment.* T. A. Bevis, 1982.

BEVIS, Trevor A. *Hereward, the siege of the Isle of Ely and involvement of Peterborough and Ely monasteries together with 'De Gestis Herewardi Saxonis', the exploits of Hereward the Saxon.* T. A. Bevis, 1981.

BEVIS, Trevor A. *Fenland saints and shrines and associated places.* T. A. Bevis, 1982.

BLOOM, Alan. *The skaters of the Fens.* Heffer & Sons, 1958.

BOWLES, Bill. *The memoirs of a Fenland mole catcher.* Cambridgeshire Libraries, 1986.

CHAMBERLAIN, Mary. *Fen women: a portrait of women in an English village.* Routledge, 1983.

CORY, R. H. *Fenland lighters and horse knockers.* EARO, 1978.

CROSSLEY-HOLLAND, Kevin. *Dead moon and other tales from East Anglia and the Fen country.* Faber, 1986.

DARBY, H. C. *The changing Fenland.* C.U.P., 1983.

DARBY, H. C. *The drainage of the Fens.* 2nd ed. C.U.P., 1956.

DARBY, H. C. *The medieval Fenland.* David & Charles, 1940 (reprinted 1974).

DAY, Anthony. *Turf village: peat diggers of Wicken.* Cambridgeshire Libraries, 1985.

DIXON, George. *Old Scarlett.* Annakin Fine Arts, 1980.

FRASER, Antonia. *Mary, Queen of Scots.* Weidenfeld & N., 1969.

GODWIN, Harry. *Fenland: its ancient past and uncertain future.* C.U.P., 1978.

HARRIS, L. E. *Vermuyden and the Fens: a study of Sir Cornelius Vermuyden and the Great Level.* Cleaver-Hulme Pr., 1953.

HEATHCOTE, J. M. *Reminiscences of fen and mere.* Longmans, 1876.

HILLS, Richard L. *Machines, mills and uncountable costly necessities: a short history of the drainage of the Fens.* Goose & Sons, 1967.

JOHNSON, C. *The Ely and Littleport riots ... 1816.* Harris Newsagent, Littleport, 1893 (reprinted 1981).

LINDLEY, Keith, *Fenland riots and the English revolution.* Heinemann Educational Books, 1982.

MARLOWE, Christopher. *Legends of the Fenland people.* E. P. Publishing, 1926 (reprinted 1976).

MASON, A. J. *An introduction to the Black Fens.* 2nd ed. H. J. Mason, 1984.

MATTINGLEY, Garrett. *Catherine of Aragon.* Cape, 1942.

MILLER Samuel H. and SKERTCHLY, Sydney B. J. *The Fenland, past and present.* Leach & Son/Longmans, 1878.

ORFORD, Lord. *Voyage round the Fens in 1774.* 1868.

PARKER, Anthony and PYE, Dennis. *The Fenland.* David & Charles. 1976.

PEACOCK, A. J. *Bread or blood: the agrarian riots in East Anglia: 1816.* Gollancz, 1965.

PHILLIPS, C. W. ed. *The Fenland in Roman times.* Royal Geographical Society, 1970.

RANDELL, Arthur. *Fenland Molecatcher.* Routledge, 1970.

STOREY, Edward. *Portrait of the Fen country.* 3rd ed. Hale, 1982.

STOREY, Edward. *Spirit of the Fens.* Hale, 1985.

SUMMERS, Dorothy. *The Great Level: a history of drainage and land reclamation in the Fens.* David & Charles, 1976.

WENTWORTH-DAY, James. *A history of the Fens.* Harrap, 1954.

WILLS, Norman T. *Woad in the Fens.* 3rd ed. N. T. Wills, 1979.

INDEX